H[illegible] To Handle Your Mum

By Roy Apps

Illustrated by Nick Sharratt

Hippo

Amy Bellamy

Scholastic Children's Books,
Commonwealth House, 1–19 New Oxford Street,
London WC1A 1NU, UK
a division of Scholastic Ltd
London ~ New York ~ Toronto ~ Sydney ~ Auckland
Mexico City ~ New Delhi ~ Hong Kong

First published by Scholastic Ltd, 1994

ISBN 0 590 55499 9

Printed by Cox & Wyman Ltd, Reading, Berks.

15 17 19 20 18 16 14

!!! Warning !!!

The information contained in this book can be highly dangerous if it falls into the wrong hands, i.e. your mum's.

To prevent this from happening you should take one of the following precautions:

1 Memorise every word in the book and then eat it.*[v]

2 If you are a girl, disguise the nature of this book by cutting out the next page and sticking it on the cover.

3 If you are a boy, disguise the nature of this book by cutting out the next page but one and sticking it on the cover.

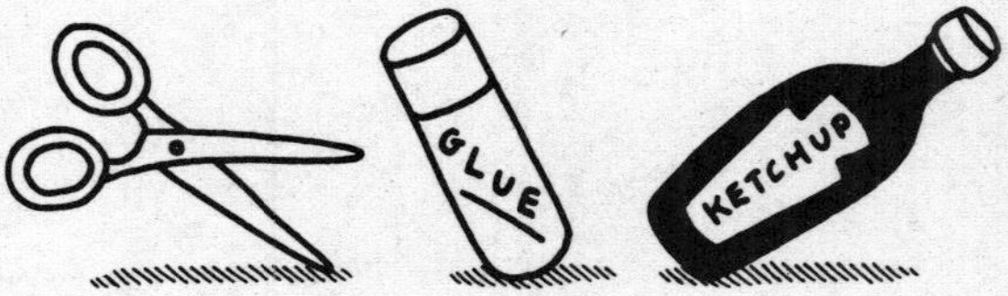

---

* *TV cook Kevin Bowtie suggests you try the following recipe if you do decide to eat this book.* Extra Whopper Book Burger: *(i) Place book in a stale sesame seed bun. (ii) Place book-filled bun on paper napkin. (iii) Add two tablespoons of extra hot chillies. (iv) Eat (the bun, not the napkin).*

[v] *This book is suitable for vegetarians.*

1001 Ways to Become a Perfect Daughter

By Gladys Goodchild

Cut along the dotted line

1001 Ways to Become a Perfect Son

By Norbert Neverude

Cut along the dotted line

Contents

STAGE 1 Why it is important to be able to handle your mum – NOW! 11

STAGE 2 Finding out just what kind of mum you've got 16

STAGE 3 Finding out if your mum is an alien 21

STAGE 4 What makes mums different? 24

The Next Chapter 28

STAGE 5 The five superhu-mum powers and how to combat them 30

1 Radar Ear 30
2 Gamma-Ray Eye 41
3 Laser Tongue 47
4 Athlete's Leg 52
5 Game Boy Brain 56

STAGE 6 Training your mum 61
1 The Training Program 61
2 Training Your Mum to Stop Being Nosey 66
3 Training Your Mum to be Reasonable 69
4 Training Your Mum not to Embarrass You in Public 71

STAGE 7 Using a Secret Agent..................... 74
1 Grannies 74
2 Ghouls 77
3 Gerbils 81

STAGE 8 The Mum-handling Test 84

STAGE 9 Compiling your own Mum-handling Data Bank... 89
1 File One – Data On Your Mum............... 90
2 File Two – Data On Your Mum's Superhu-mum Powers 93
3 File Three – Additional Data 96

How To Handle Your Mum: Stage One

Why it's important to be able to handle your mum – NOW!

Ask yourself this question:

What's the difference between your mum and a mountain bike with square wheels and 57 reverse gears?

Tricky one, this, so here's a picture to help you.

Look at the gears on that bike – what a laugh! Now look at the gear on that mum – what an even bigger laugh! But to get back to the question: your mum isn't like a mountain bike with square wheels and 57 gears, because *you can't take her back to the shop you got her from and ask them for a model that's easier to handle*. You've got to learn to handle the mum you got when you were born.

It's important to be able to handle your mum *now*, because the older you get, the more difficult it becomes. In fact, the only people who don't need to learn how to handle their mums are newborn babies. They've got it (or rather her) completely and absolutely worked out. Take the following scenes. Done that? Now put them back in the book and read them!

Scene 1

YOU: *(Slamming the front door behind you and yelling at the top of your voice)* Hey, Mum! *Mum!!!* I wanna Coke!

YOUR MUM: Come back in again like a civilised human being, speak properly and remember the little word . . .

YOU: *(Coming in again, this time closing the door quietly and speaking in hushed tones)* Mum? Could I have a Coke, please?
YOUR MUM: No, you can't. We're just about to have dinner.
(*Result:* You don't get your Coke.)

Scene 2

NEWBORN BABY: *(Hammering fists on Mum's chest)* Yahhh!!!! Bahhhh!!! Woooo!!!! YEEAAAGHHH!!!
MUM: Ooo . . . my little darling. Do you want a drink?
(*Result:* Baby gets a drink.)

Scene 3

It is half past nine in the morning. You are lying down on your bed, taking a well-earned, post-breakfast rest, kind of half-dozing, half-daydreaming about how much better your life will be when you finally become a World-Beating Number One Sports Superstar. Suddenly a hurricane blasts into the room. It's –

YOUR MUM: Oh, for goodness' sake, *(insert your name here)*! Get up, you great schlummock and go and do something useful like learning to play the clarinet or hoovering your room or visiting your grandmother. (*Result:* Either you learn to play the clarinet, tidy up your room and visit your grandmother, or you reach a compromise and learn how to hoover up your grandmother with a clarinet.)

Scene 4

It is half past nine in the morning. The newborn baby is lying down in its cot, taking a well-earned rest, half-dozing, half-daydreaming under its Spot the Dog mobile. Suddenly a kind and gentle breeze wafts into the room. It is –

MUM: Aaahhhh . . . Does my little darling want to go to sleepy-byes? (*Sings*) Bye, Baby Bunting, etc., etc.

(*Result:* Baby is left on his/her own to do whatever he/she wants until it's time for another drink. [See Scene 2.])

So there you have it. There are two methods open to you of handling your mum. Either you can go back to being a baby again and start wearing nappies, or you can read this book. Which method do you fancy? Tricky decision, eh? You probably need two seconds to decide. So here they are:

ONE SECOND

ANOTHER SECOND

Made your choice? OK, for those of you who have decided to become babies again, I hope you'll have a nappy time! Don't forget you'll need a dummy too. On second thoughts, you won't need a dummy, because you probably *are* one.

For those incredibly intelligent and sensible people who have decided to learn how to handle their mums by reading this book, the first thing you must do is this: TURN OVER!

How To Handle Your Mum: Stage Two

Finding out just what kind of mum you've got

Just what kind of mum have you got? There's a very simple answer to this, which is – How on earth do you expect *me* to know? You've never even introduced me to her.

There are only three kinds of mums who are easy to cope with. And there aren't many of them left. These mums are rather like blue whales and African elephants, in other words they are an endangered species.*

Type 1: The Mummy-Type Mum
An incredibly ancient mum originating from North-East Africa and known as an Ancient Egyptian Mummy.

** According to wildlife expert, Dr David Bellamummy.*

They look like this:
If your mum is this kind of mummy, I've only got one thing to say to you: I hope you take after your dad!

(Typical Mummy-Moan: "Have you been cleaning your bike chain in the kitchen sphinx *again?*")

Type 2: The Mother-Type Mum
A mum who thinks she's the best thing since Super Nintendo and who therefore likes to be called Mother or, more correctly, *Mother Superior*. They look like this:

If your mum looks like this, tell her to stop buying her clothes from the local convent's jumble sales.

(Typical Mother-Superior Saying: Nun.)

Type 3: The Mama-Type Mum
Mums who are dead posh like to be called Mama (pronounced Mar-Mar), which is short for Mar-Ma-Ladies. They look like this.
If your mum is one of these Mar-Ma-Ladies, she will be very easy to handle. Just keep her on the top shelf in the larder and only bring her out at meal times.

(Typical Mar-Ma-Lady Saying: "Use a spoon to get me out of the jar, not a knife!")

The chances are that your mum is neither an Ancient Egyptian, nor a nun, nor a jar of orange jam, so learning how to handle her is going to be rather like conjuring, in other words, a very *tricky* business.

Fortunately, help is at hand. To be more precise, help is *in* your hand in the form of this book. For the first time in the history of mankind – and more importantly of *mum*kind – a giant mainframe computer has been designed to provide answers to some of the most difficult problems people have with their mums. It's called the MUMBO (stands for MUMs had Better watch Out) JUMBO.

Now, it's a well-known scientific fact that mums aren't like any other sort of people. So first of all, an incredibly brilliant computer programmer* fed millions of megabytes of data into the MUMBO JUMBO to try to discover what kind of mum I had. After spending years reading the data, the MUMBO JUMBO eventually flashed this message up on the screen:

** This incredibly brilliant computer programmer is also incredibly modest and won't reveal his name. However, you can find out who he is by rearranging the following letters: E M.*

I fell off my seat. I was stunned. (This was because I banged my head on the desk.)

"First of all find out what planet she's from?" I said.

"Are you sure?" I asked.

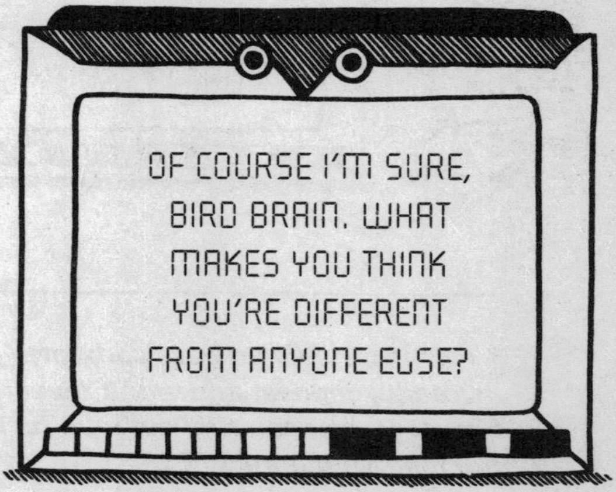

How To Handle Your Mum: Stage Three

Finding out if your mum is an alien

Complete the following questionnaire to find out what kind of alien your mum is.

1. Does your mum ever say (or think) any of the following to you:

a) "I think you . . .

☐ . . . watch too much telly."

☐ . . . have far too much pocket money."

☐ . . . go to bed far too late."

b) "I don't think you . . .
☐ . . . get enough homework."
☐ . . . understand the meaning of tidiness."
☐ . . . eat enough cabbage."

2. Does your mum think Sonic the Hedgehog is:
☐ a kiddie's cartoon series
☐ your favourite band
☐ a small prickly creature who lives at the bottom of your garden?

3. Does your mum think any of the following are the height of fashion?
☐ school blazers
☐ anoraks
☐ hand-knitted pullovers
☐ vests?

4. Does your mum reckon any of the following people are right on/cool/well smart?

☐ Cilla Black
☐ The woman who reads The News (any of them)
☐ The bloke who reads The News (any of them)
☐ Seb Coe?

If you've ticked any one of the above questions, then ask yourself, *where on earth* has your mum been living for the past five years?

To which the answer must be . . . *nowhere on earth*. Therefore she must be an alien.

To which there is a very obvious question . . . "Which planet does she come from?"

To which there is a very obvious answer . . . "Ma(r)s."

How To Handle Your Mum: Stage Four

What makes mums different?

Once I'd discovered that my mum was an alien, a lot of things began to fall into place. Like why she calls my dad "Hunkikins" when she thinks I'm not listening, when really his name is Eric. ("Hunkikins" is obviously the alien translation of Eric.) But that still didn't explain just why mums are *so* difficult to handle. I asked the MUMBO JUMBO to explain.
And the MUMBO JUMBO said:

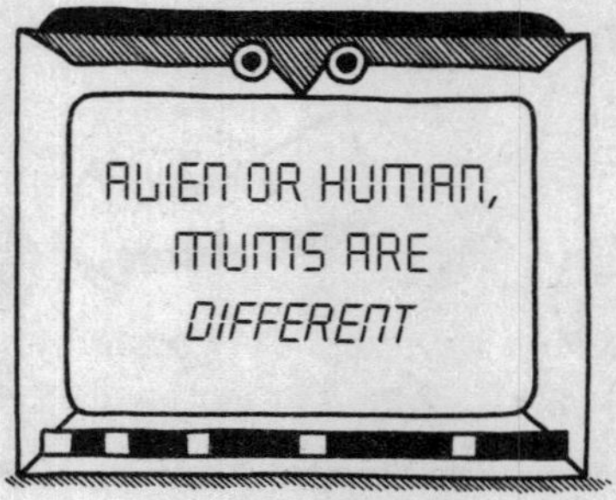

So I asked the MUMBO JUMBO what it is that makes mums different from other aliens and humans.

And the MUMBO JUMBO said:

I said, "Could've told *you* that!"
And the MUMBO JUMBO replied:

I asked the MUMBO JUMBO *why* having children made mums different.

And the MUMBO JUMBO replied:

** In case you were thinking, "What about dads?", dads don't* have *children. They just acquire them once they are born.*

The MUMBO JUMBO had obviously got a computer virus. So I put it to bed with a mug of hot honey and lemon and when it felt better it said this:

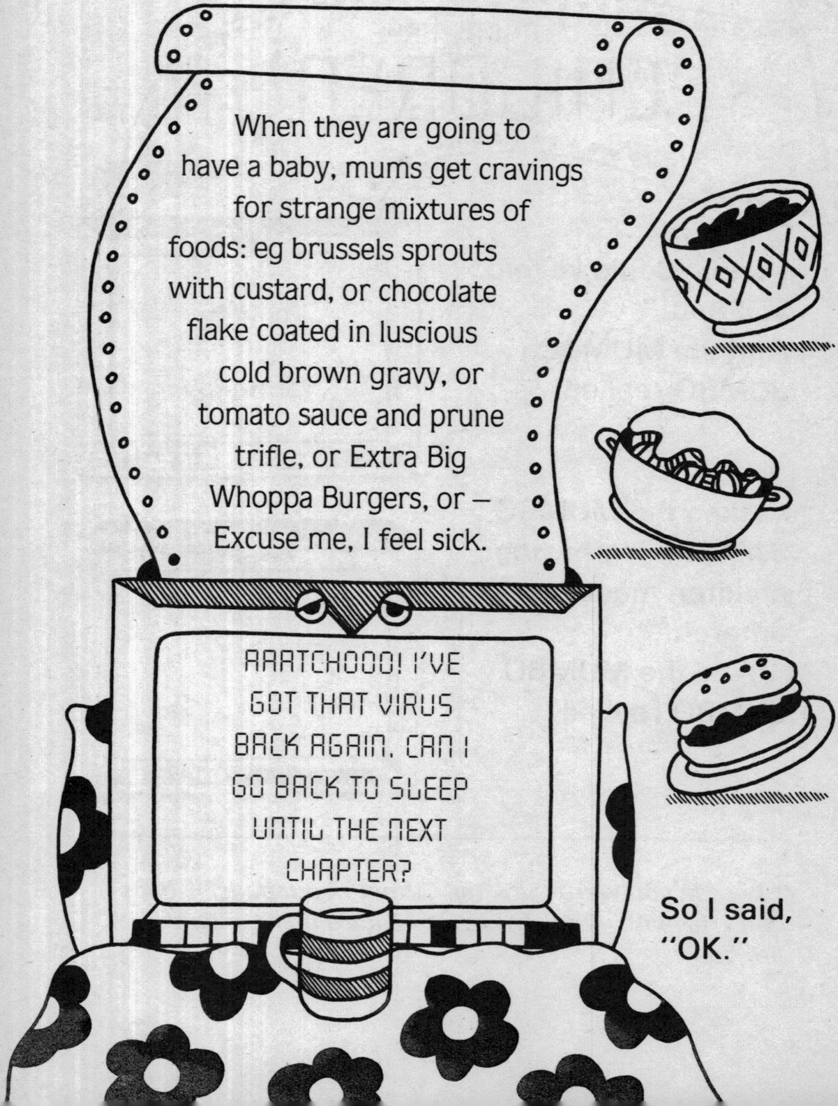

So I said, "OK."

And the MUMBO JUMBO said:

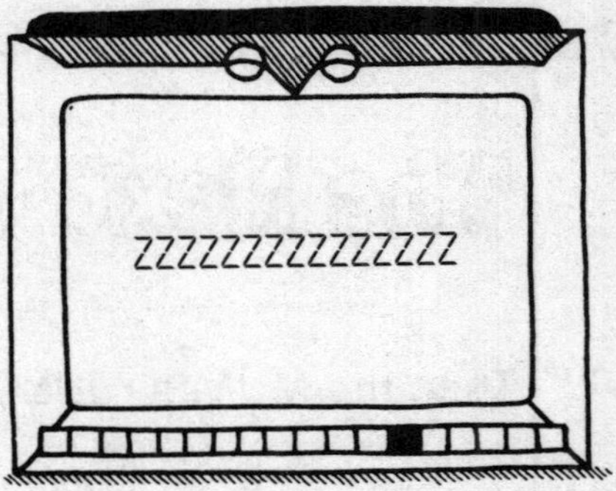

I said, "Wake up!"

And the MUMBO JUMBO said:

I said, "This *is* the next chapter."

And the MUMBO JUMBO said:

So I said, "Oh, yes it . . .

The Next Chapter

. . . is."

Then the MUMBO JUMBO said:

So I said,
"Oh, blow it!"

And it did.

And this is what it said next:

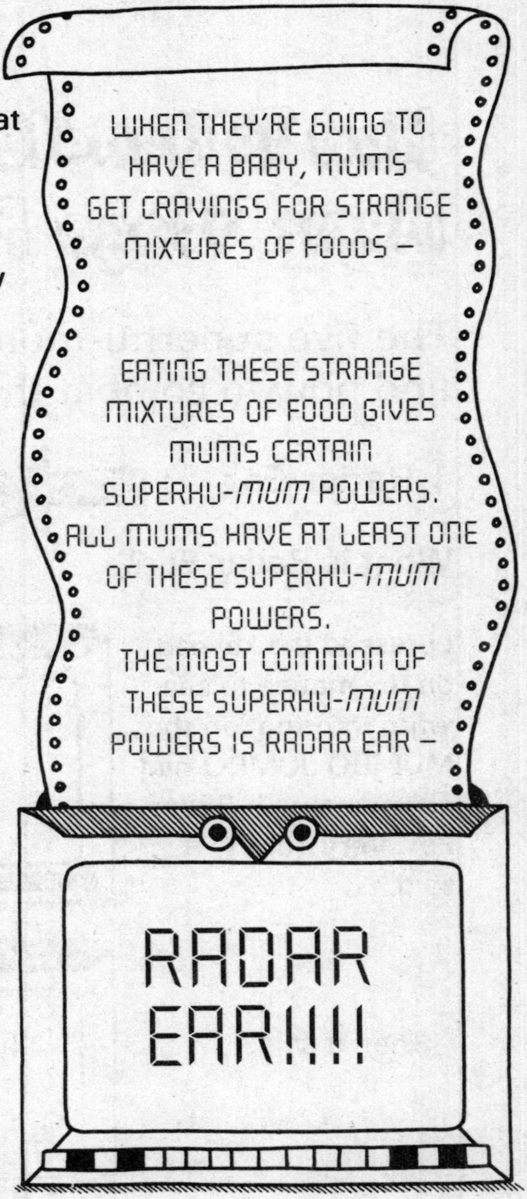

"Yes, we know all that."

"Pardon? I didn't quite catch that . . ."

How To Handle Your Mum: Stage Five

The five superhu-mum powers and how to combat them

1 Radar Ear

What is Radar Ear?

I pressed the keypad on my mouse to see what information the MUMBO JUMBO had on mums with Radar Ear. Very quickly it said:

Then it said:

And I suddenly realised what the problem was. The MUMBO JUMBO was scared of my mouse. It leapt up onto the top shelf of my bookcase and there it stayed. Luckily I've got a back-up computer. It's called My Brain. So here is everything I know about mums with Radar Ear.

An ordinary ear looks like this:

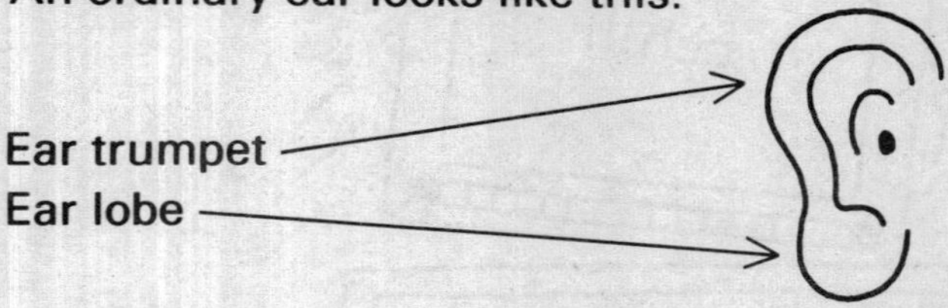

A mum's Radar Ear looks like this:

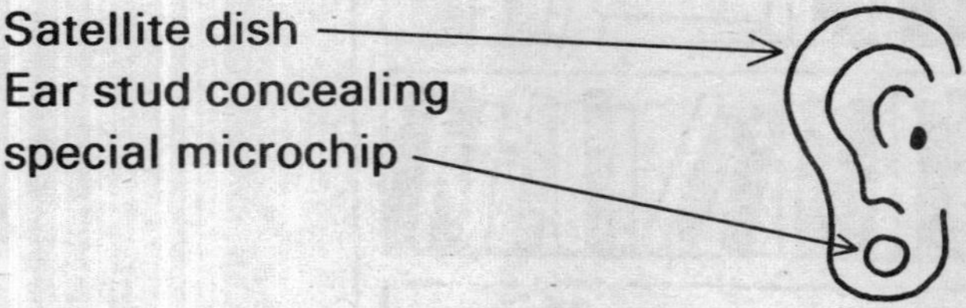

The kind of things mums with Radar Ears tend to say are:
"*I hear* that the Queen's coming to open the new by-pass."

Now, did that mum actually go to Buckingham Palace and hear the Queen say: "Philip! Ay'm just orff to open the new Clogbury bay-pass. Ay've left you a boil-in-the-bag kipper for your supper."

Of course not. Rather, she was just about to give the cat its Whiskas when she decided to turn her Radar Ear in the approximate direction of London SW1 and, so powerful is a mum's Radar Ear, she heard what the Queen was saying to Prince Philip without any difficulty whatsoever.

When your mum comes to use her Radar Ear on you, however, it works in a particularly devilish way. It can actually decide what to pick up and what not to. It picks up everything you *don't* want your mum to hear, and it cuts out anything you *do* want her to hear.

I asked the MUMBO JUMBO to explain and it said:

So I did. And the MUMBO JUMBO came up with the following table:

I said,
"That's a very old joke."

And the MUMBO JUMBO replied:

Then the MUMBO JUMBO came up with this table:

Words and phrases of yours that a mum's Radar Ear always picks up	*Words and phrases of yours that a mum's Radar Ear never picks up*
"*!$!*$!!" (that is, any word that is at all rude.)	"I'd like (a) a 20-gear mountain bike, (b) a horse and stables in the back garden for my birthday, please."
"No, of course my mum won't mind if we look after your pet tarantula for the holidays."	"Can we go to Disneyland for our holiday this year?"
"Chomp, chomp!" (tucking into the Black Forest Gateau that's thawing specially for your mum to take to the school Parents' Association dance.)	"Can Karen and I go to the Take That concert at Wembley Stadium, please?"

You can work out how good your mum's Radar Ear is by conducting the following experiment:

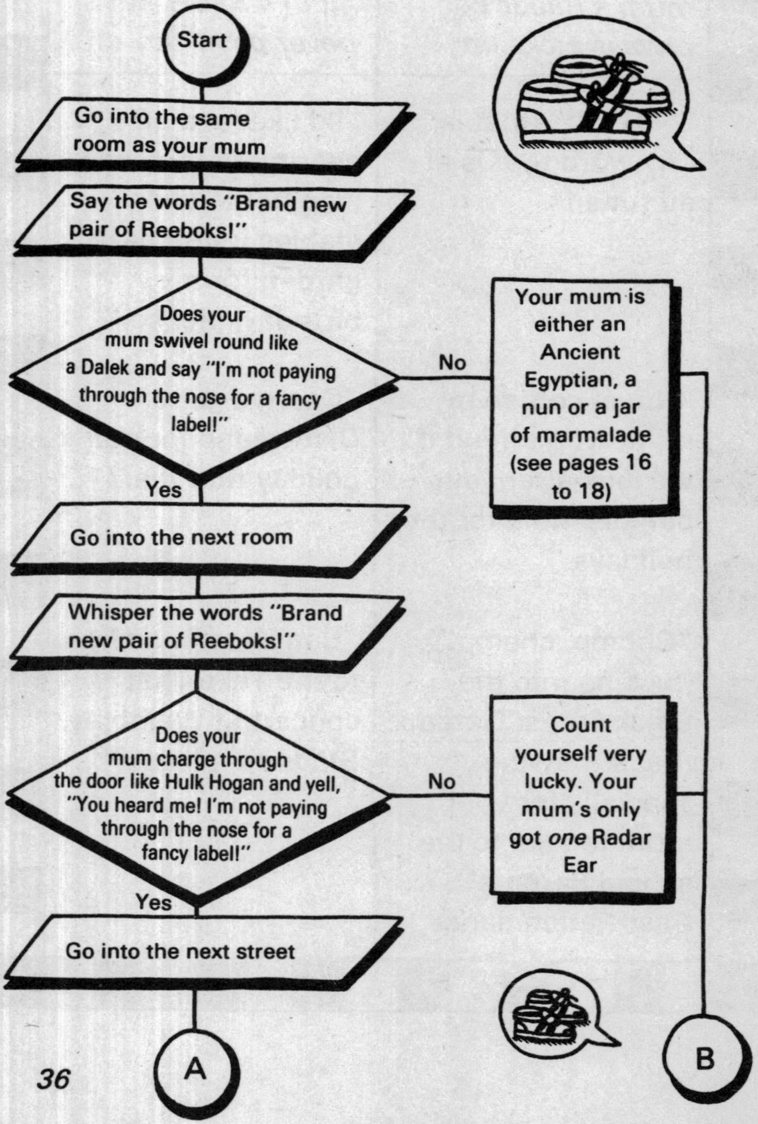

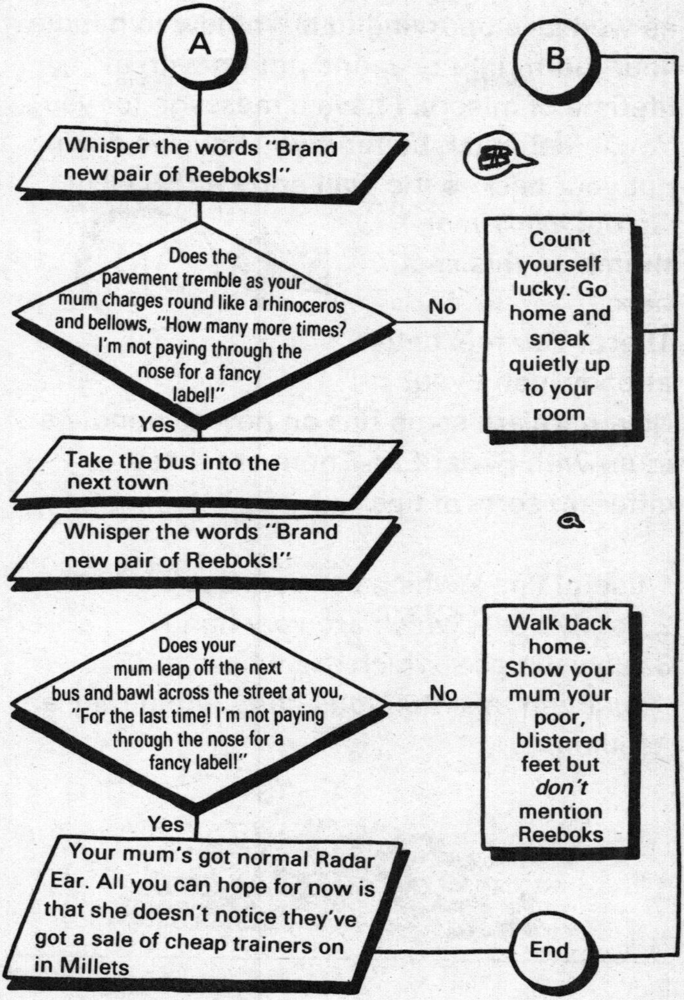
A
B
Whisper the words "Brand new pair of Reeboks!"
Does the pavement tremble as your mum charges round like a rhinoceros and bellows, "How many more times? I'm not paying through the nose for a fancy label!"
No
Count yourself lucky. Go home and sneak quietly up to your room
Yes
Take the bus into the next town
Whisper the words "Brand new pair of Reeboks!"
Does your mum leap off the next bus and bawl across the street at you, "For the last time! I'm not paying through the nose for a fancy label!"
No
Walk back home. Show your mum your poor, blistered feet but *don't* mention Reeboks
Yes
Your mum's got normal Radar Ear. All you can hope for now is that she doesn't notice they've got a sale of cheap trainers on in Millets
End

If you think things look so bad that you might as well give up trying to learn how to handle your mum right now and put up with a lifetime of misery, I have a message for you. You'll feel much better if you knuckle down, put your back to the wall and PRESS ON!!*

Go on! With your thumb on this spot here:

There! You feel better already, don't you?

Now here are some tips on how to handle a mum with Radar Ear. There are three different sorts of tips:

1 useful tips – which are very useful
2 handy tips – which are very handy
3 rubbish tips – which are where the dustmen take their dustcarts when they are full up.

** On the other hand, if you get confused and press down with your knuckles on the wall, you could end up feeling a lot worse – not to say in need of several bits of sticking plaster.*

How to handle mums with Radar Ear

1 The Satellite Solution. Give your mum and her Radar Ear something else to listen to other than you. The most obvious thing to do is to strap her to the chimney, so that her Radar Ear can operate as a satellite dish. I say this is obvious, because if your mum is strapped to the chimney, she certainly will be (obvious, that is).

Advantage of this solution: The rest of your family will be really pleased with you, because they'll be able to watch Premiership soccer on Monday nights.

Disadvantage of this solution: With your mum strapped to the chimney, you'll have to get your own tea.

2 The Ear Muff Method. Knit your mum a pair of really thick woolly ear muffs. She'll be so touched by your thoughtfulness that she'll wear them all the time you're around.

Advantage of this method: You won't have to get your own tea.

Disadvantage of this method: Have you ever *tried* knitting a pair of ear muffs?

3 The Semaphore Solution. Instead of talking, you could use semaphore. This is a system of communication that uses flags, so it is completely silent and can never be picked up by Radar Ear or any other sort of ear for that matter.

Advantage of this solution: You could earn extra pocket money by hiring yourself out to local fêtes as a flag pole.

Disadvantage of this solution: Limited as a means of communication – have you ever tried doing semaphore while riding a bike or cleaning your teeth, for example?

2 Gamma-Ray Eye

What is Gamma-Ray Eye?

asked the MUMBO JUMBO.
"If I am, are you going to tell me the answer?" I replied.

The MUMBO JUMBO said:

So I gave it a silicon chip sandwich.

It took a couple of megabytes and said:

Gamma-Ray Eye enables your mum to actually see *through* things. For example, to anyone else your bed looks like this:

But to a mum with Gamma-Ray Eye, it looks like this:

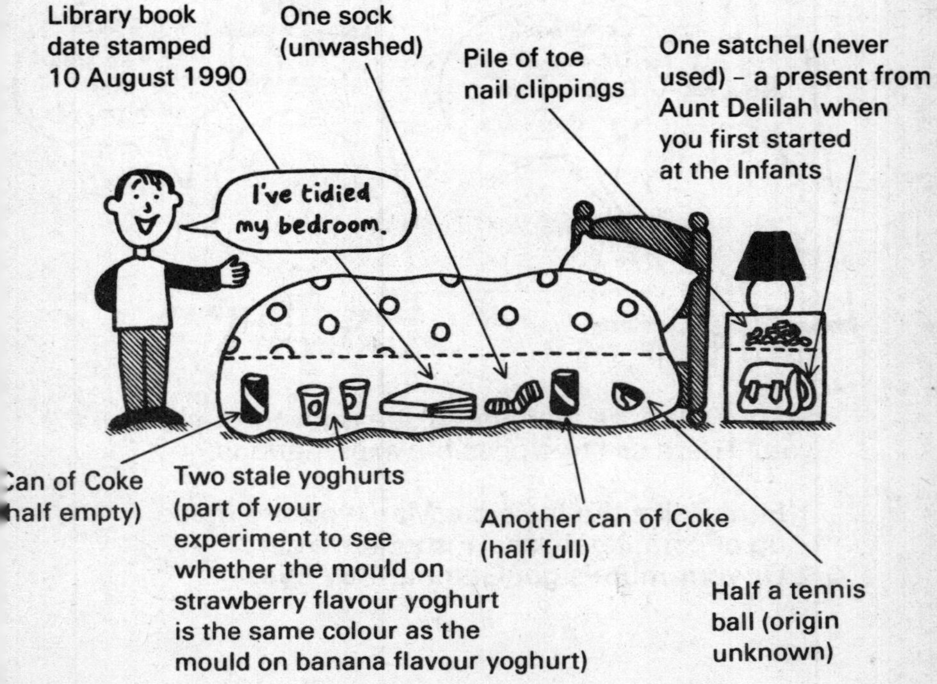

Another problem comes when you're leaving the house. You're halfway to the front door with your back to your mum, but she calls out:

If you're a boy

If you're a girl

So how did she manage to see right through you? There are two possible explanations:

1 Either, like the Invisible Man, you are made up of completely see-through matter;
2 Or your mum's got Gamma-Ray Eye.

How to handle mums with Gamma-Ray Eye

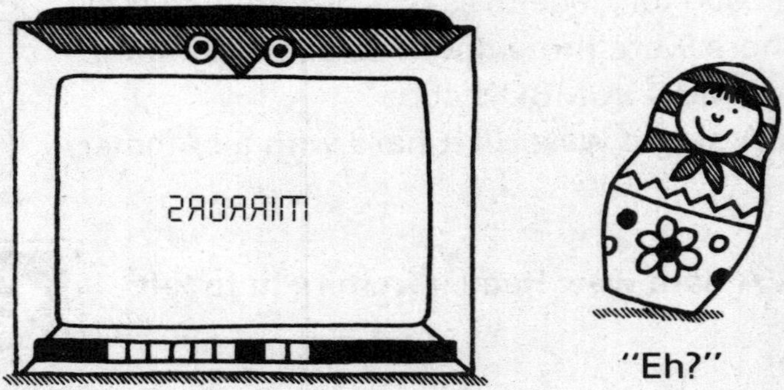

At first I thought the MUMBO JUMBO had suddenly learnt to speak Russian, then I realised this tip on how to deal with Gamma-Ray Eye was so secret, the MUMBO JUMBO would only reveal the details in code. What I needed was a code breaker.

So I looked in the *Yellow Pages* under C for Code Breakers. It said: *Turn to* Z

I did. And found Zoob Glakers plc, which is a code for Code Breakers plc. They told me there were three methods of breaking the MUMBO JUMBO's code:

1 A stupid way: Hit it hard with a hammer.

2 A hard way: Read it from right to left.

3 An easy way: Place a mirror along the left-hand side of the page.

OK, readers. Choose your method and break the code.

HANDLING GAMMA-RAY EYE

IF THERE'S ANYTHING YOU

DON'T WANT YOUR MUM TO SEE

MAKE SURE YOU ARE HOLDING A

MIRROR UP IN FRONT OF HER FACE

What happens, of course, is that the Gamma-Rays are directed straight back at your mum. Elpmis, isn't it?

3 Laser Tongue

What is Laser Tongue?

Sharp, cutting and deadly – that's what a mum's Laser Tongue is. It enables them to come out with really devastating comments. Here are some examples:

(When you've tried to clean your bike by putting it in the dishwasher): "You've got as much brain as a bowl of blancmange."

(When you've asked for the umpteenth time if you can have a pony for your birthday): "Why on earth do we need a pony when we've already got a donkey?" (She means you.)

(When you've just put on your brand new Take That CD): "Oh, no! Sounds like the cat's got trapped in the tumble drier again!"

Laser Tongue works on a Pick 'n' Mix principle. Your mum will pick a target then choose a suitable laser-tongued phrase to describe it. See if you can pick 'n' match these targets to the right Laser Tongue phrase.

Common targets of mums' Laser Tongues	*Common phrases of mums' Laser Tongues*
Your incredible brain power	about as much use as a chocolate hammer
Your exquisite table manners	two gherkins short of a Big Mac
Your favourite actor/singer	as much taste as a second-hand herbal tea bag
Your superb taste in TV programmes	picked up in the Safari Park
Your keen clothes sense	looks like a herd of wildebeest have just stormed through it
The state of your room	makes a sack of spuds look chic
Your amazing ability to stand on your head for seven and a half minutes without being sick	like Frankenstein's monster, but without his charm

How to handle mums with Laser Tongues

The MUMBO JUMBO said:

And I said, "Any more talk like that, and I'll start using that mouse again!"
So the MUMBO JUMBO said:

I said, "Thank you very much."
Then I realised that this was the MUMBO JUMBO's handy hint on how to handle your mum's Laser Tongue. (i.e. be like Ken* and *creep*.)

This is how it works:
MUM: Why on earth do we need a pony when we've got a donkey? (*See above*.)
YOU: Oh, Mum! Why on earth do we need a pony when we've got a donkey! Oh, how clever . . .! How witty –
MUM: Do you really think so?
YOU: Oh, yes. Ha, ha, ha! Ho, ho, ho!
MUM: It *was* rather good, now you come to mention it. Ho, ho, ho!
YOU: Ha, ha, ha! I wish I could be as witty as that!
MUM: I bet you do! Ho, ho, ho!
YOU: Ha, ha, ha! You *are* going to let me have a pony, aren't you, Mum? You're so clever, Mum!
MUM: Yes, of course I am, dear!
YOU: Thank you very much, Mum!

---

* *Full name: Ken-I-do-that-for-you-miss-please-miss, aka the teacher's pet.*

4 Athlete's Leg

What is Athlete's Leg?

Compared with a mum's speed as she catches you sneaking out for a game of football without having first tidied your room, Linford Christie is about as fast as a snail with a zimmer frame. Compared with a mum's speed as she catches you sneaking up to your room without first having put your dirty dinner plates in the sink, Sally Gunnell is about as fast as a tortoise with bricks in its boots.

Yes, Superhu-mums are *fast*. The really clever thing, though, is that they don't *look* fast. That's why it's so easy to be taken by surprise. It's all to do with clothes.

On top your mum might look like this:

But *underneath*, she'll be wearing something like this:

In fact, in your mum's eyes, your house is nothing more than an athletics stadium.

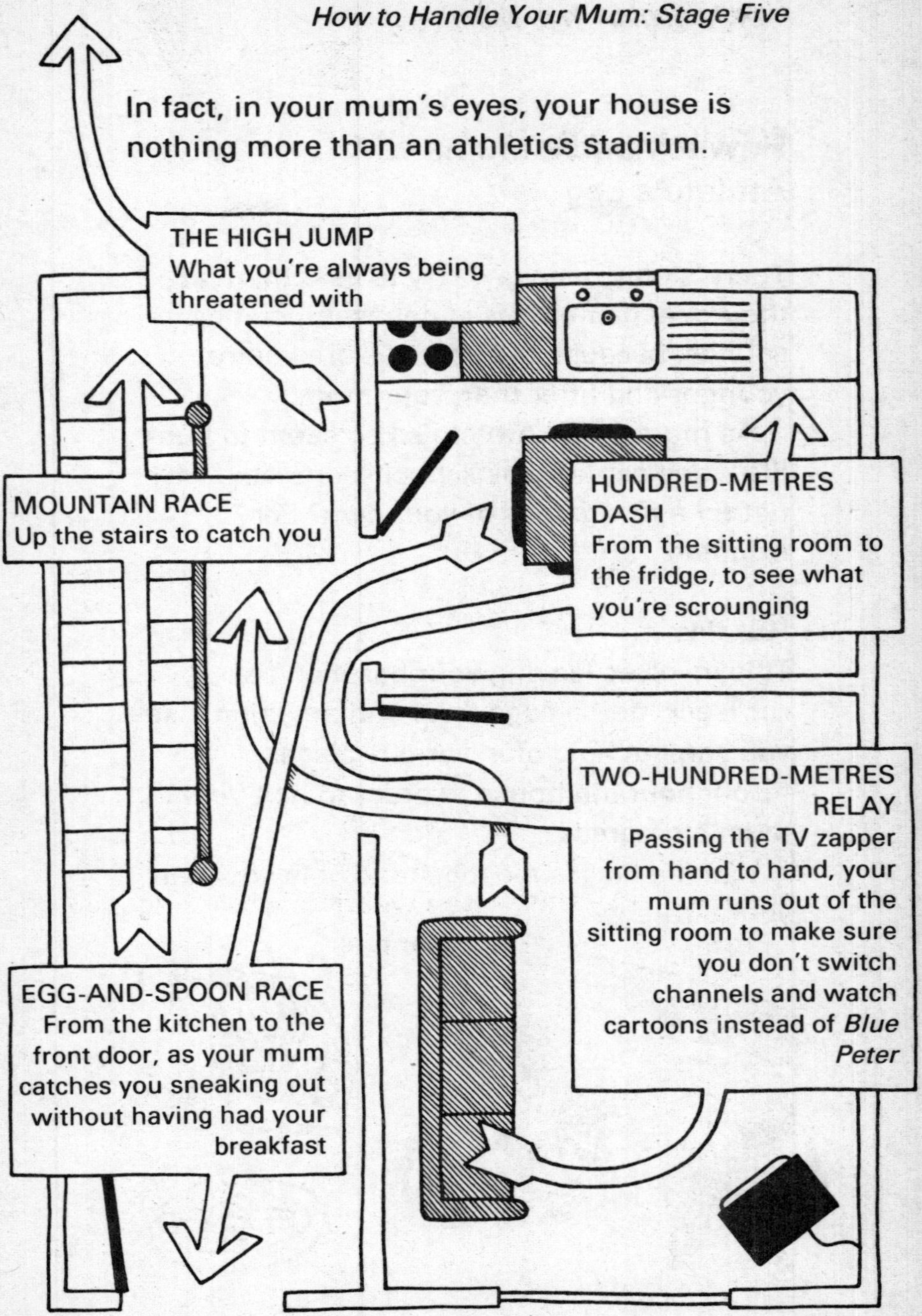

How to handle mums with Athlete's Leg

There's only one way – try to beat them at their own game. This is not as difficult as it sounds, because the chances are you're younger and fitter than your mum.

As mums with Athlete's Leg seem to think life's one continuous school sports day, why not try a few games of your own? For example:

Hurdles
This involves leaving your baseball bat, rucksack, gerbil cage, bike and anything else you can get hold of in various places throughout the house in order to halt your mum's progress.

Use the diagram opposite to help you plan your strategy.

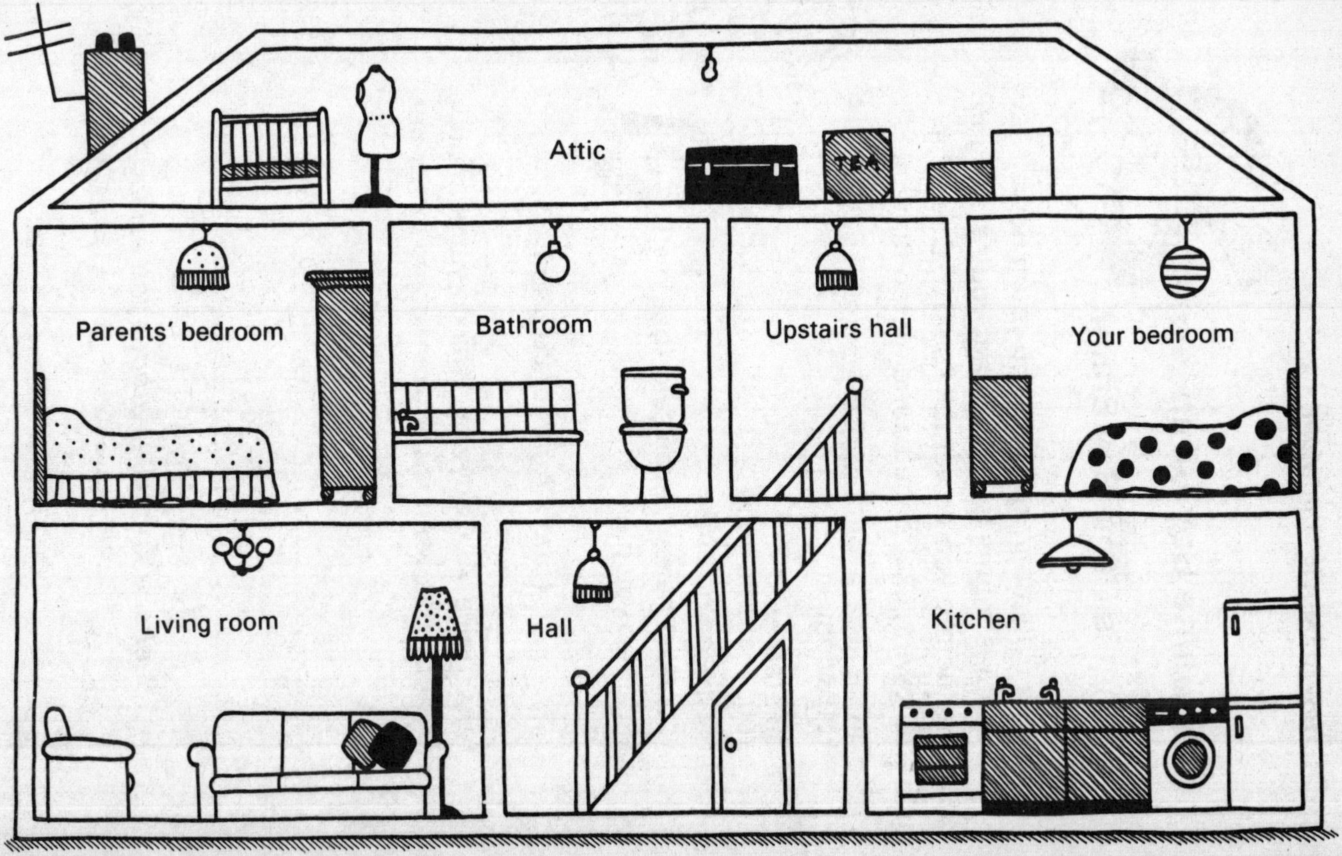
Attic
TEA
Parents' bedroom
Bathroom
Upstairs hall
Your bedroom
Living room
Hall
Kitchen

5 Game Boy Brain

What is Game Boy Brain?

This truly amazing Superhu-mum power enables mums to know what you're going to say before you've actually said it. Does the following exchange sound all too familiar?

YOU: Mum . . .
MUM: No, you can't.
YOU: Just this once . . .?
MUM: And no buts.
YOU: But I haven't even said "but" yet!
MUM: Yes you have.

(*She's right, of course!*)

MUM: Twice. And anyway, why do you want to *(insert whatever it is you were going to ask her for)*

....

....

(See! she knows – without you asking!)

YOU: Oh, go on, Mum! Please! If you let me, I'll –

(You're about to say "I'll take the dog for a walk for you," when your mum butts in.)

MUM: Dad took it through the car wash yesterday.

(Yahoo! Jubilation! You've got her this time, you think! Her Game Boy Brain has failed her! She thinks you were going to offer to wash the car, rather than take the dog for a walk!)

YOU: Dad took our dog Rover through the car wash?
MUM: No, Dad took our car Rover through the car wash.

YOU: I wasn't going to offer to wash the car, Mum. I was going to offer to take our dog for a walk. That surprised you, didn't it? Eh?
MUM: It certainly did. We haven't got a dog!

(You are about to crawl up to your room, totally and utterly defeated in your request, when your mum strikes the killer blow.)

MUM: OK!
YOU: OK what, Mum?
MUM: You've been very good about the house lately, so I'll let you – just this once. Now run along.

(At this point you realise with a sickening feeling that, what with all the argy-bargying with your mum, you've completely forgotten what it was you'd asked her for in the first place! So you continue crawling up to your room, totally and utterly defeated.)

How to handle mums with Game Boy Brain

I asked the MUMBO JUMBO for advice on this most tricky of all the Superhu-mum powers and it said:

Which is another way of saying, write the following letter:

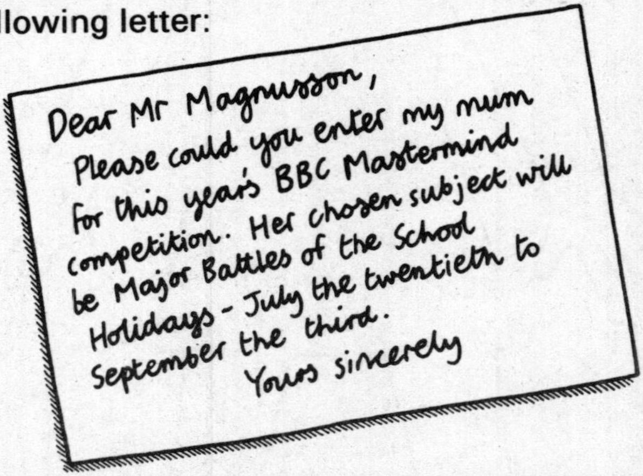
Dear Mr Magnusson,
Please could you enter my mum for this year's BBC Mastermind competition. Her chosen subject will be Major Battles of the School Holidays – July the twentieth to September the third.
Yours sincerely

Once entered as a "Mastermind" contestant, your mum will have to start learning to answer questions *after* she has heard them and not before.

FOR YOUR OWN REFERENCE, INSERT DETAILS OF YOUR MUM'S SUPERHU-MUM POWERS HERE:

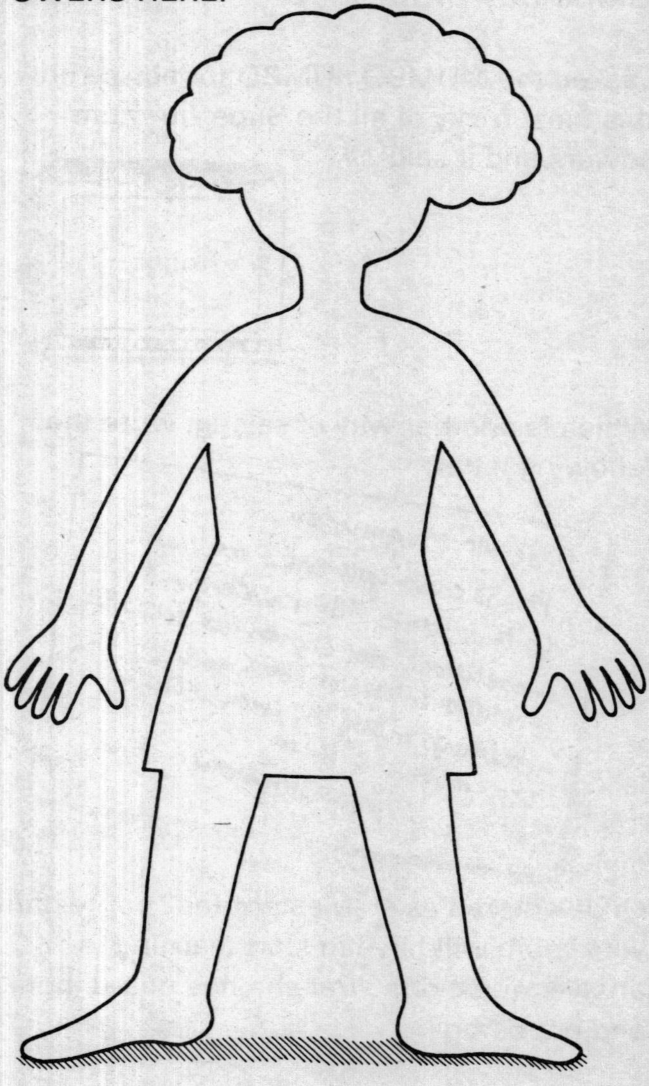

How To Handle Your Mum: Stage Six

Training your mum

1 The Training Program

Now that you've learnt about Superhu-mum powers and have practised dealing with them, you should be in a position to progress to Stage Six – training your mum.

To undertake this training, you will need the help of a decent *trainer*. Trainers are very flash people with fat, soft bottoms and they gave their name to a particular type of running shoe.

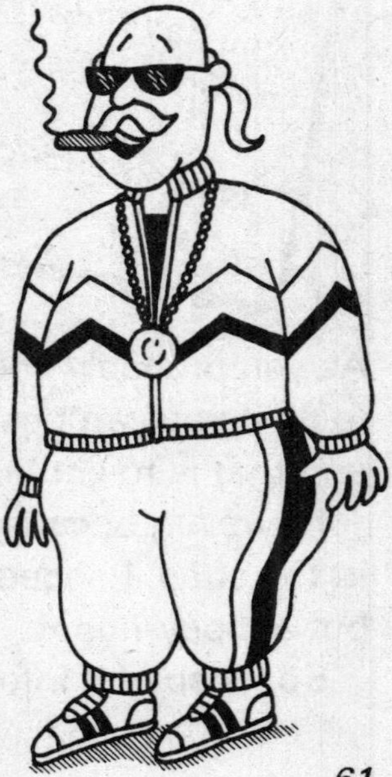

However, when I asked the top trainer in the country for his advice on the Training of Mums, he sent me this very *cross* letter. It was:

Then he sent me another very cross letter:

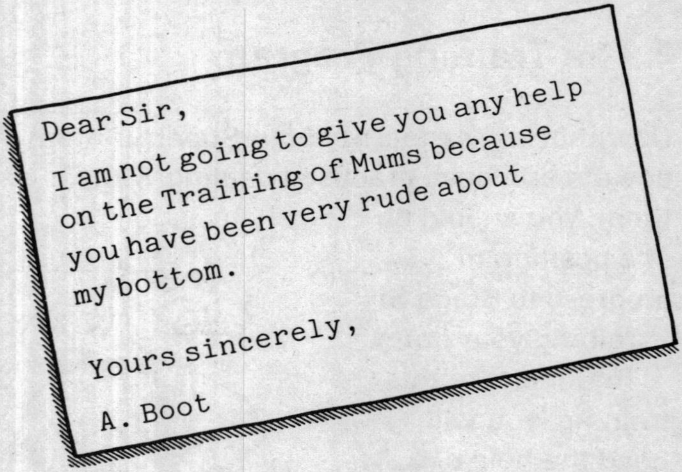

Dear Sir,

I am not going to give you any help on the Training of Mums because you have been very rude about my bottom.

Yours sincerely,

A. Boot

As you probably know, there is only one thing to do if you can't get hold of a decent trainer, and that is to get hold of a decent flip-flop.

However, because of a misunderstanding in the shop, I ended up not with a flip-flop, but a flippy-floppy.

So I loaded it into the MUMBO JUMBO.

And the MUMBO JUMBO said:

Obviously, the training of mums is a ticklish subject. Then it said:

THE TRAINING PROGRAM:
COMPLETE THE FOLLOWING DATA:

1 Is your mum older than you? YES/NO

2 Is your mum a woman? YES/NO

If your answer to both of the above questions is YES, proceed:*

3 Does your mum expect you to go to bed
(a) before the Ten o'Clock News
(b) after the Ten o'Clock News
(c) before *Emmerdale?*

** If your answer to either Question 1 or Question 2 is NO, then contact one of the Sunday newspapers immediately and offer to sell them your story for a huge sum of money.*

4 During school holidays, does your mum let you stay in bed until
(a) lunchtime
(b) *Home and Away* time
(c) sunset?

5 You're off school sick. You ask your mum if you can watch TV. Does she say
(a) If you're too ill to go to school, you're too ill to watch telly
(b) Yes, but only schools telly
(c) Yes, but only quiz shows?

6 You ask your mum if you can start a football club, using your back garden as your home ground. Does she say
(a) And what about the greenhouse windows?
(b) Only if you appoint me manager
(c) Yes, of course you can?

How to score:

3 a: One point
b: Another point
c: Lucky you – have you ever seen *Emmerdale*? It's a lot less interesting than being asleep in bed.

4 a: One point
b: Another point
c: Your mum thinks you're a vampire.

5 a: Minus twelve points
b: No point at all, really
c: Your mum thinks your illness has gone to your brain.

6 a: Minus ten points (and minus ten windows)
b: Half a point. At least if she's the manager she won't be able to be the ref
c: You obviously haven't got a back garden.

Score: Over three – see your teacher about taking extra Maths. Under three – join the club. You have got a mum who is *unreasonable*.

2 Training Your Mum to Stop Being Nosey

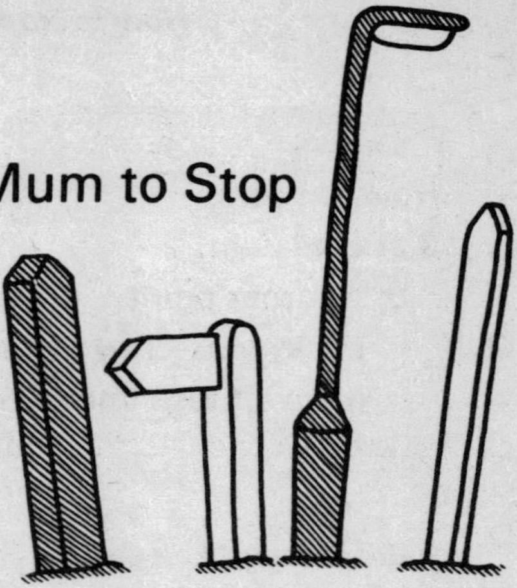

When I came to look in my postbag on this subject, I found these:

Well, what else do you expect to find in a *post* bag? Oh, all right! There were lots of letters too, every one of which had been opened and read. By my Mum, of course. Here is one of them:

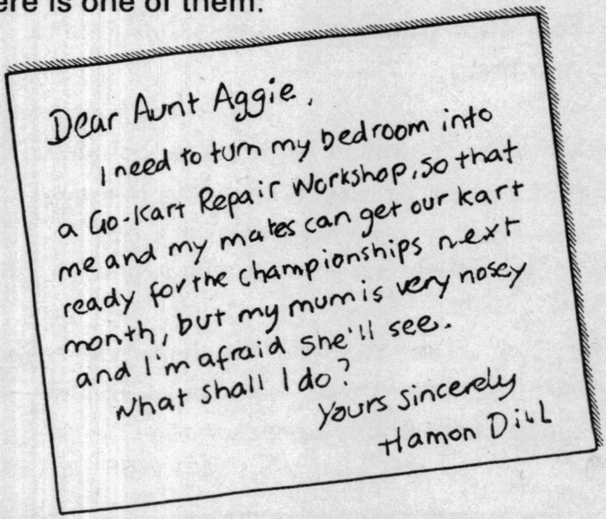

Dear Aunt Aggie,

I need to turn my bedroom into a Go-Kart Repair Workshop, so that me and my mates can get our kart ready for the championships next month, but my mum is very nosey and I'm afraid she'll see.

What shall I do?

Yours Sincerely

Hamon Dill

I fed this letter into the MUMBO JUMBO and it replied:

And I said, "Of course it's not! It's a pseudonym I use when I'm writing my Agony Aunt column."

"Yes."

So I did.

So that was that one solved! Then I looked at the next letter in the postbag. It read:

Dear Aunt Aggie,

The red herring idea was no use. My mum's a vegetarian.

Yours Sincerely,

Hamon Dill.

So I replied:

Dear Hamon Dill,

Make your own red herring using the inside of a toilet roll tube and an old coat hanger. Then say to your mum, "No! No! Please don't look in my room!" She will naturally think you've got something to hide. She storms in – and sees the red herring. "Ooh, isn't that nice!" she says. "I thought for one nasty moment you were trying to conceal a Go Kart Repair Workshop in here!" She won't bother being nosey for at least a week – time enough for you to set up a Go-Kart Repair Workshop in your room.

Yours,

Aunt Aggie

P.S. Alternatively you could take up Formula One Racing instead.

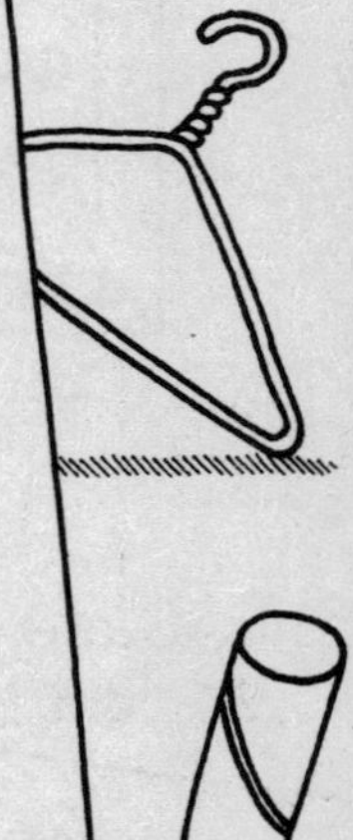

3 Training Your Mum to be Reasonable

There is a very popular saying amongst mums:

"Oh, for goodness' sake, (insert name here)! Be reasonable!"

And of course, you are – all the time. Unfortunately, training *mums* to be reasonable can be very difficult indeed. It involves going Over The Top or, as it is more commonly known, "going O.T.T." Here are a couple of typical case histories.

Case History Number One

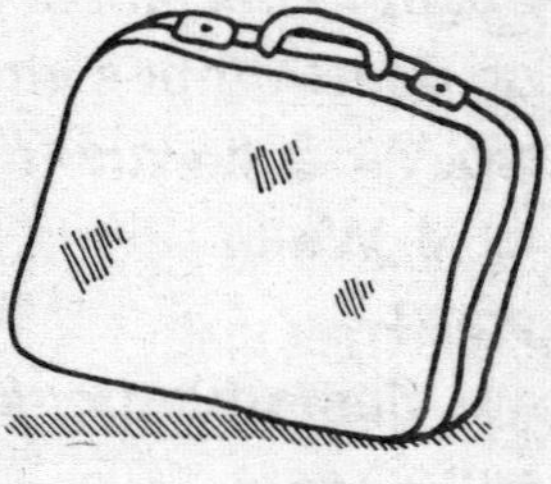

The history of this case is that it was made in 1966 by a Mr Reginald Arkwright of Northampton, and after an utterly uneventful life, turned up as an illustration in this book in 1994.

Case History Number Two

Mo Rapping wants to go and buy the new CD by her favourite group, Got This. Her mum, though, thinks the only singer suitable for a ten-year-old girl to listen to is Cliff Richard. So Mo goes O.T.T. and pretends she's into Heavy Metal . . .

MO: Mum, can I go to the Squidgy Bogies concert?
MUM: *(Shaking with terror)* For goodness' sake, Mo! Be reasonable! They're Heavy Mental!
MO: Heavy *Metal* – that's right, Mum. They really blow your brains out.
MUM: *(Terrified that her darling daughter is about to become a Heavy Metal Freak)* Oh dear, oh dear! What's wrong with *decent* music?
MO: What do you mean, "decent music"?
MUM: Well . . . er . . . not Heavy Metal, for a start!
MO: Something *quieter*?
MUM: Yes . . .

MO: Like Got This, do you mean?
MUM: (*sighs*) Look, if I let you get the Got This CD, will you promise never ever to mention going to see the Squidgy Bogies again?
MO: Of course, Mum.

See? Easy, isn't it?

4 Training Your Mum not to Embarrass You in Public

It's as natural (and as unpleasant) as goat's yoghurt for your mum to embarrass you in public.

When I asked the MUMBO JUMBO why this should be so, it said:

But I shouldn't advise you to go hunting through your mum's make-up bag to find it. Because what with her Gamma-Ray Eye and Game Boy Brain, she's bound to catch you. If you're a girl this could be very awkward, and if you're a boy it could be awkward, embarrassing, totally humiliating and an utter disaster.

The most common way for people to avoid being embarrassed by their mums in public is to *hide*.

Hiding your face

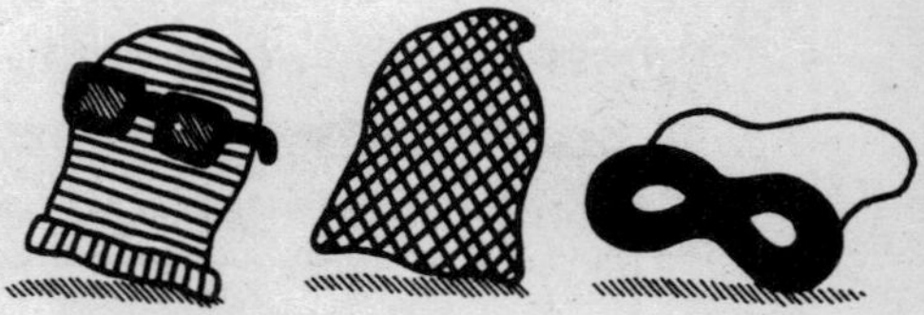

Ever wondered why bank robbers wear stocking masks? It's nothing to do with them not wanting to be seen by the security cameras, it's simply that they got fed up with their mums coming up to them in the banks they were robbing and saying things like:

"Ronnie! Get back home immediately and finish your breakfast. I've made bread-and-butter soldiers for you, specially."

Just hiding . . .

Try walking six paces behind your mum, when you're out with her. Then when she says to Mrs Noggin from five doors down: "Doesn't he take after his Aunt Vera?" you can duck behind the nearest tramp and Mrs Noggin will assume your mum is referring to a passing Rottweiler.

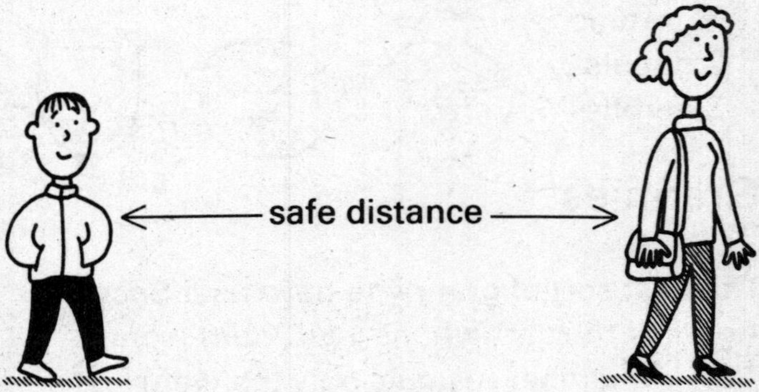

However, hiding won't do anything to *cure* the problem. You really must try to *train* your mum to stop embarrassing you in public, and the only way to do this is to use *a Secret Agent* . . .

How To Handle Your Mum: Stage Seven

Using a Secret Agent

The Secret Agents you use to help you handle your mum are so-called because you keep it a secret from them that they are working for you.

There are three types of Secret Agent who are worth seeking out to help you with your work:

1 grannies
2 ghouls
3 gerbils

Grannies

The best sort of granny to have as a Secret Agent is the sort who is your mum's mum. They remember (usually only too well) just what your mum was like when she was your age.*

** Yes, incredible though it may seem, your mum was once a fun-loving, sensitive, totally reasonable young person like yourself!*

This, as we will see later, can be very useful indeed.

You may already know of the exploits of the most famous Granny Secret Agent of them all. If you do, it can mean only one thing – you've read this book before . . .

Granny Bond sat in her armchair watching snooker on the telly. There was a knock at the door. In walked her granddaughter, Brooke Bond.

"Oh, Granny Bond, you've got to help me to handle my Mum!"

"Let's just call her M, shall we?" said Granny Bond. "Is she being embarrassing in public again?"

"You bet!" said Brooke.

"What's she done this time?"

"It's not what she's *done*, it's what she *wears!* Fluorescent purple and orange leggings, an old baggy sweater and beads in her hair."

"Ah! Your mum thinks she's being *cool*," explained Granny Bond.

"Cool! I should think she's freezing!" said Brooke.

"Ssshhh!" said Granny Bond, "Here comes your mum now!"

In came Brooke's mum, dressed in her fluorescent purple and orange leggings, baggy sweater and beads.

"Georgina!" said Granny Bond. "You are *not* going out looking like that!"

"But, Mum!" said Brooke's mum.

"Go upstairs and change," said Granny Bond. "You've got as much taste as a second-hand herbal tea bag!"

"That phrase sounds familiar," said Brooke.

"It should do," replied Granny Bond. "It's on page 49 of this very book!"

And thanks to Secret Agent Granny Bond, Brooke's mum never ever embarrassed her in public again by wearing her purple and orange leggings, her old sweater and beads.

Ghouls

The best kind of ghouls to use as Secret Agents are those who blow gum in old ladies' faces, swear, spit, spray Darren 4 Karen on lampposts, pass wind during school assembly and generally behave very badly indeed. There is probably at least one in your class.

Boy ghoul

Girl ghoul

Now, you may think "I'd rather suffer years of torture at the hands of my Mum, than have to talk to the likes of Lenny Lickspittle or Felicity Foulmouth," but the beauty of using a ghoul as a Secret Agent is that you don't have to talk to them at all!

The way it works is like this: your mum absolutely hates this sort of ghoul. When she mentions such people her voice takes on a tone that makes Lord Snooty sound like somebody out of *EastEnders*.

"You don't sit next to *Lenny Lickspittle* in class, surely?"

"Come away from the front window! That *Felicity Foulmouth* is passing the house."

Your mum is absolutely terrified that you will end up the next Lenny Lickspittle or Felicity Foulmouth! So here's an example of how to use a ghoul as a Secret Agent:

(Scene: *Your local department store. Your mum is buying you a new coat. Her eyes light upon a dreadful anorak thing that looks as if it was last worn by Postman Pat's granny. But there's no doubt about it – your mum thinks it's just the thing for a girl like you.)*

MUM: It certainly looks as if it will *last.*
(You have visions of this anorak still not being worn out by the time you leave school. Meanwhile, you have your eyes on a rather natty zip-up jacket. Time to use your Secret Agent.)

YOU: Oh, Mum! You wouldn't make me wear *that* anorak?
MUM: And why not? I suppose it isn't "cool", is that it?
YOU: No, it's definitely not "cool", as you put it.
MUM: Huh!
YOU: And the reason it's not "cool" is that it's just the sort of coat Felicity Foulmouth would wear!
MUM: *(horrified)* Is it?
YOU: Definitely!
MUM: Oh, dear!
YOU: I don't want to go around looking like Felicity Foulmouth, do I?
MUM: *(with feeling)* Er, no . . . You most certainly do not.
(Steer your mum in the direction of the natty zip-up jacket.)

Gerbils

All schools have a pet gerbil. These harmless little creatures sit around all day without much to do, so you might as well employ them as Secret Agents. They can be used in a similar way to ghouls.

Your mum probably doesn't hate the school gerbil in the same way as she hates Felicity Foulmouth and Lenny Lickspittle, but she's terrified of having the poor little thing in the house. She's afraid that it will escape, or even expire while it's under your roof. If that happened, of course, she would die of shame because the neighbours would all avoid her in the street and the RSPCA would set up an undercover round-the-clock watch on your house. So here's an example of how to use the school gerbil as a Secret Agent in the battle to handle your mum:

(Scene: *the kitchen. The problem: Your best mate Steve has invited you to go with him and stay at his cousin's for a weekend. His cousin lives a few miles from Alton Towers!*)

MUM: *(showing typical superhu-mum powers)* No, you can't go away for the weekend.
YOU: But, Mum! Steve's invited me. Wouldn't it be rude to say no?
MUM: It's the Community Association car boot sale on Sunday. I was relying on you to give me a hand.
(Yee-oww!!! This is even more serious than you thought! You'd forgotten about the dreaded Community Association car boot sale. Time to call in your Secret Agent.)

YOU: *(sigh)* Oh, well. I suppose Old Soggy* will be pleased.
MUM: Why should Mrs Sponge** be pleased?
YOU: It means we'll be able to have the class gerbil for the weekend after all.
MUM: *(White with fear)* What? Eh? Er, no . . . Yes, of course you can go with Steve to his cousin's for the weekend!
(Time to go upstairs and start packing your rucksack.)

** Your class teacher's nickname*
*** Your class teacher's real name.*

How To Handle Your Mum: Stage Eight

The Mum-handling Test (Key Stage 2)

Test your knowledge of mums and how to handle them in this specially designed quiz from the MUMBO JUMBO computer program.

1 Which of the following are superhu-mum powers?

- ☐ a Runny Nose
- ☐ b Radar Ear
- ☐ c Pain In the Neck
- ☐ d Gamma-Ray Eye
- ☐ e False Teeth
- ☐ f Laser Tongue
- ☐ g Knobbly Knees
- ☐ h Athlete's Leg
- ☐ i Game Boy Brain

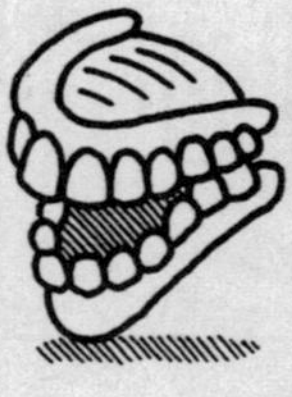

2 Which of the following will help you in training your mum?

☐ a A packet of dog biscuits

☐ b A flock of sheep

☐ c A Secret Agent

3 Who would be likely to cause you more embarrassment if you found yourself with them in the local shopping precinct?

☐ a Jeremy Beadle

☐ b Your mum

☐ c Donald Duck

4 Your mum tells you your room is a mess and starts fuming. Do you

☐ a Ring the fire brigade?

☐ b Buy a mirror?

☐ c Tidy it up?

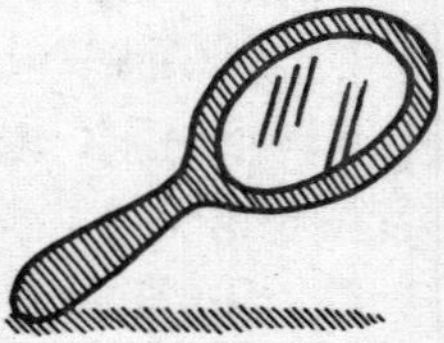

5 Which of the following is a rare type of mum?

☐ a David Bellamummy
☐ b A Thingamummy
☐ c A jar of orange jam

6 What do computers believe is the source of mums' superhu-mum powers?

☐ a Inter-galactic energising electrons from the planet Glurg
☐ b A handbag
☐ c Food

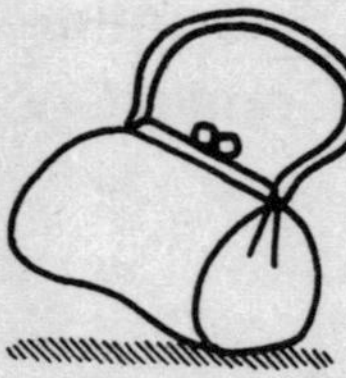

7 Why did the chicken cross the road?

☐ a To get to the other side
☐ b Because it was egged on
☐ c To avoid being embarrassed by its mum in public

8 Which of the following things should you *never* say to your mum?

☐ a "What did you do in the war?"

☐ b "Is that one of Grannie's dresses you're wearing?"

☐ c "Your home-made burgers are almost as good as McDonald's."

9 How old is your mum likely to wish you were?

☐ a Old enough to know better

☐ b Old enough to buy a car

☐ c Two and a half

10 What is the name for an occasion when your mum and your friends' mums all get together for a chat?

☐ a A coffee morning

☐ b A hen party

☐ c Nightmare on Elm Street

Answers

1. 1 point each for numbers b; d; f; h; i. Half a point for e (False teeth). This is a Superhu-*gum* power.
2. 1 point for c. 1 point for b (providing your mum is Little, her first name is Bo and your surname is Peep).
3. 1 point for b. If you put down a, You've Been Framed.
4. 2 points for b and 999 for the fire brigade.
5. 2 points for c and a 1000 whatsitsnames for thingamummy.
6. 2 points for c. If you put b, then I'd like to know just what you were doing looking in your mum's handbag.
7. 1 point for c. Nothing whatsoever for b – it's one of the very worst jokes I have ever heard.
8. None of them! Take away a hundred points for each thing you thought you could say to your mum.
9. Deduct 50 points for b. Score 1 point for a (every mum says this at least once a day). Score 2 points for c. All mums like to think they're a lot younger than they are, which they would be if you were still two and a half!
10. They might *call* it a or b, but of course it's c. Score 2 for c.

Your Score

Minus 1050 or more? You'll find the Samaritans' number in the phone book.

Between minus 1050 and 10? OK, you know the theory, now go out and practise it!

Between 10 and 19½? Glad I'm not your mum!

More than 19½? You can't count.

How To Handle Your Mum: Stage Nine

Compiling your own Mum-handling Data Bank

Keeping a personal data bank about your mum-handling is vital, but you must make sure to keep it in a place that's safe from your mum's Gamma-Ray Eye. (Like a reinforced steel box buried in two-foot-thick concrete.)

PERSONAL DATA BANK

CONFIDENTIAL

NAME:______________

DATA ON YOUR MUM

File 1:

Basic Statistical Data

How many jobs has she got? ....

(Going out to work counts as one job, looking after you and any brothers and sisters you may have counts as four jobs)

Height..

Width ....

Weight ....

(Vital information for dealing with her Athlete's Leg powers)

Age (How old she actually *is*) ....

(See opposite)

Bartering/Bribery/Buttering Up Data

How old she would like you to think *she is*..

Other soft points, i.e. What she likes to be complimented on (Her brains/cooking/looks/driving/incredible wit/collection of Abba records [see below])

....

Favourite group ....
(You can impress your mum by saying how good they are, or by naming some of their hit singles – if they ever had any)

Favourite TV programme ....
(So that you know what is positively the very worst time to try and handle her, i.e. while it's on)

Favourite brand of chocolates ....

There are certain days in the calendar when buttering up can work especially well. These days are:

Mother's Day (date varies) ....

Your mum's birthday (date)...........................

CONFIDENTIAL

Your birthday (date) ....

Phobias (i.e. spiders/snakes/your sweaty trainers)...

Her attitude to you

What she calls you when she's cross with you ....

What she calls you when she's really *cross with you* ....

The person in your class she most wishes you were more like ....

The person in your class she's most glad you aren't like...
(See p.77: Using Ghouls as Secret Agents)

What she wants you to do when you leave school...

CONFIDENTIAL

CONFIDENTIAL

NAME:________________

DATA ON YOUR MUM'S
SUPERHU-MUM POWERS

File 2:

Radar Ear

The longest distance from which your mum can pick up the noise of anything you shouldn't be saying or doing (in kilometres) ....

Gamma-Ray Eye

The thickest substance your mum can see you through:

Quite thick substance (bucket of sludge) YES/NO

Really thick substance (bucket of stodgy custard*) YES/NO

Really really thick substance (two buckets of stodgy custard*) YES/NO

Unbelievably thick substance (your big brother's/sister's head) YES/NO

** Available from your school cook.*

Laser Tongue

The usual word your mum calls you when she's cross with you, using the N Index (words beginning with N)

Nerd	YES/NO
Nincompoop	YES/NO
Nigel	YES/NO
Nitwit	YES/NO
N.E. Other?	....

Athlete's Leg

Your mum's running style when she chases you upstairs to your room. Does she:

Hop like mad	YES/NO
Run like crazy	YES/NO
Leap like a frog that's sat on a firework?	YES/NO

Game Boy Brain

Work out your mum's Game Boy Brain IQ by:
Adding her age to the number of teeth she's got ....
Subtract the number of records she's got by Cliff Richard ....
Multiply by the number of times a day she says "When I was your age" ....

Your mum's Game Boy Brain IQ is....................

NAME: ____________

ADDITIONAL DATA

File 3:

Secret Agents:

Name ....
Code name ....

Name ....
Code name ....

Name ....
Code name ....

Name ....
Code name ....

Name ....
Code name ....

CONFIDENTIAL